24 Lessons
Vol. 2

A Practical Method to
Learn the Art of Cello Playing

Martin Stanzeleit and Chihiro Takeuchi

Contents

Lesson Movies

http://www.martinstanzeleit.com/24lessons/24videos/e-videolist.html

Attic Room

http://www.martinstanzeleit.com/24lessons/yaneura/yaneura.html

Lesson 13
Meeting the Big "B"

Get dressed and better see that your fingernails are cut and clean. Polish your cello, tune the strings, and put some rosin on your bow. One last look into the mirror and you are ready to meet the big "B" – Johann Sebastian Bach, sometimes called the father of all cello music. Bach was one of the first composers to have recognized the potential of the cello as an independent solo instrument. Up to the 18th century, the cello had its place supporting and accompanying other instruments. Great luthiers of the time, first and foremost Antonio Stradivarius, managed to improve the sound and playability of the cello vastly by shortening its size. More and more, composers picked up on the idea of writing solo pieces for the cello. Alessandro Scarlatti and Domenico Gabrielli among several other Italian Baroque composers were the first to designate pieces to the solo cello before the newfound reputation crossed the Alps and the mighty Bach took up his quill.

Bach wasn't all that mighty in his time – when he applied for the post of cantor for the St. Thomas Church in Leipzig, he came only fifth. The four others in line ahead of him all withdrew, giving Bach the opportunity to step up. The rest, of course, is history.

To play Baroque pieces on the cello, you need to be very agile with both the bow and the left hand. There is an ongoing discussion about how far to render the original playing style. We won't join that discussion here, but let us agree that your bow technique should be very flexible and clean. So should your intonation be, too, by the way.

Playing broken chords is called "Arpeggio". Let us start by practising Arpeggio across the open stings. Watch this demonstration to see how arm, wrist and fingers collaborate.

[Video D 13.1: Arpeggio demonstration]

For all Arpeggio exercises of this lesson, set your metronome to ♩=60.

M 13.1a

[Video 13.1a: Open strings Arpeggio]

Now the same exercise with slurs:

M 13.1b

[Video 13.1b: Open strings Arpeggio with slurs]

Next, we add a finger on the A-string.

M 13.2a

[Video 13.2a: Arpeggio pattern 2]

Practise this and the following exercises also with slurs!

M 13.2b

[Video 13.2b: Arpeggio pattern 2 with slurs]

Now, it gets a little more difficult, because we add two fingers across the strings. When the same finger is used on two strings, you need to stretch it across before you start. Watch the demonstration to get the idea.

[Video D 13.2: Stretching a finger across two strings]

M 13.3

[Video 13.3a: Arpeggio pattern 3]
[Video 13.3b: Arpeggio pattern 3 with slurs]

Placing the second finger on the D-string makes things even trickier!

M 13.4

[Video 13.4a: Arpeggio pattern 4]
[Video 13.4b: Arpeggio pattern 4 with slurs]

Let us move on to scales. Arpeggio scales will be a staple of your warm-up routine from now on! M 13.5

Also practise these scales with slurs.

[Video 13.5a: Arpeggio scales basic pattern]
[Video 13.5b: Arpeggio scales basic pattern with slurs]

For this lesson, we chose two Etudes by Sebastian Lee, Nos. 11 and 20, which are a perfect preparation for Bach's Prelude.

♩=72

M 13.6

[Video 13.6a: Lee Etude No.11]
[Video 13.6b: Lee Etude No.11 accompaniment]

♩=76

M 13.7

[Video 13.7a: Lee Etude No.20]
[Video 13.7b: Lee Etude No.20 accompaniment]

Now we will start the Prelude of the first suite by Johann Sebastian Bach. His suites for the cello are a staple of our repertory. Even if you think it is too early to start playing such a complex piece, the idea is to improve your technique and playing ability while tackling the work bit by bit, like learning by doing.

In this lesson, we will be doing only the first half of the prelude. Let's start with a preparatory exercise that summarizes all chords of the first half. Use long bows and pay a lot of attention to your sound. Once you get going with the real thing, you will be busy with other things, so take the time to get your intonation right.

♩=56

M 13.8

[Video 13.8a: Bach Exercise No.1]

[Video 13.8b: Bach Exercise No.1 with slurs]

Again, practise also this exercise both with and without slurs.

And now, finally, it is time to get started with the real thing!

M 13.9

[Video 13.9: Bach Prelude First Half]

In order to get the basic pattern right, here are some suggestions on how to practise the Prelude.

♩=88

M 13.10

[Video 13.10: Prelude practise pattern 1]

M 13.11

[Video 13.11: Prelude practise pattern 2]

M 13.12

[Video 13.12: Prelude practise pattern 3]

Try to come up with your own ideas on how to practise the Prelude!

One point advice

Think of the first half of the Prelude as if it was a trip from harmony to harmony. Where do you reach the first minor key? Which harmonies seem to sound open and relaxed, which are tight? Which harmonies seem to invite the player to linger, which harmonies seem to push the music forward?
Try to create your individual course of events for this piece.

Summary of Lesson 13:

- Arpeggio exercises
- Arpeggio scales
- Etudes Nos.11 & 20 by Sebastian Lee
- Preparatory exercise for Bach's Prelude G-major
- Prelude from the Suite No.1 by Johann Sebastian Bach

Johann Sebastian Bach
1685 - 1750

Lesson 14
Baroque-ing on

When playing Baroque music, or even older music, you will realize that besides the notes themselves, there are not many hints on how the composer wanted his music executed. Up to Beethoven's time, it simply wasn't common to write down every instruction in detail. Of course, this doesn't mean that the composers of the time didn't want dynamic nuances or didn't care about articulation. In many instances, the composer performed his own works, and therefore knew what he wanted. In cases where the pieces were written for others, a great deal was left to the players, giving them both freedom and responsibility.

When studying Bach's Suites for the Unaccompanied Cello, we can't refer to an autograph. The only reference we have are copies of the original, the most famous being the one by Anna Magdalena Bach. The other one was made by Joseph Kellner, a pupil of Bach. Yet even their scores aren't very detailed in terms of articulation and dynamics. We have to imagine what the virtuoso players of that era did, and study as many other works by Bach to find similarities and correlations.

In the first Prelude, there is a hint on articulation by Anna Magdalena Bach, and we should try to stick to that pattern. We will practise the correct bowing before carrying on with the second half of the prelude.

Further, in order to play the Prelude to the end, we will introduce the 5th position and thus open the door to the yet unconquered territory beyond the fourth position. Exciting, isn't it?

Let's start with the 5th position. Do you remember our trusty "Anchor Points" of Volume 1? Well, they come in handy in this lesson, too. First, make sure you are settled safe and sound in the 4th position. From there it is only half a step up to the 5th position.

First, let's find the 5th position in a graph.

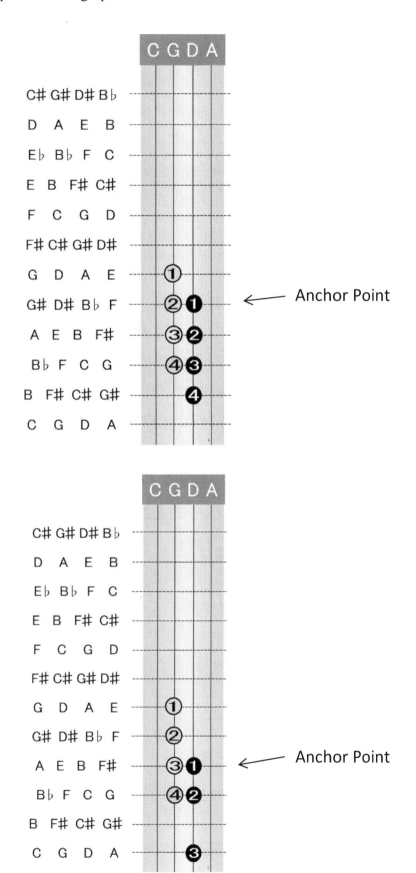

Note that the 5th position is the last position to use the fourth finger regularly. In the upper 5th position (bar 5 of the exercise 14.1), it is rather uncomfortable to place the fourth finger due to the angle of the left hand.

♩=72

M 14.1

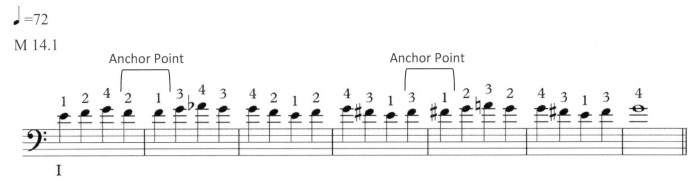

[Video 14.1: 5th position exercise]

Now, let's play the same on the D-string:

M 14.2

[Video 14.2: 5th position exercise D-string]

And now across the strings.

M 14.3

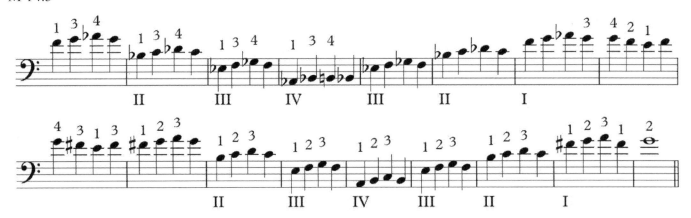

[Video 14.3: 5th position exercise across the strings]

Especially when playing on the lower strings, make sure to have a very clear sound. Without straining your hand, make sure the fingers are placed firmly on the string. Try to avoid any 'murky' sound on the G- and C-string.

There is a very convenient way to pop in and out of the 5th position by using the flageolet sound above the 4th position. Actually, the left hand doesn't perform a complete shift, the third finger is rather stretched upwards.
Watch the video to learn this frequently applied technique.

M 14.4

[Video 14.4: Flageolet technique]

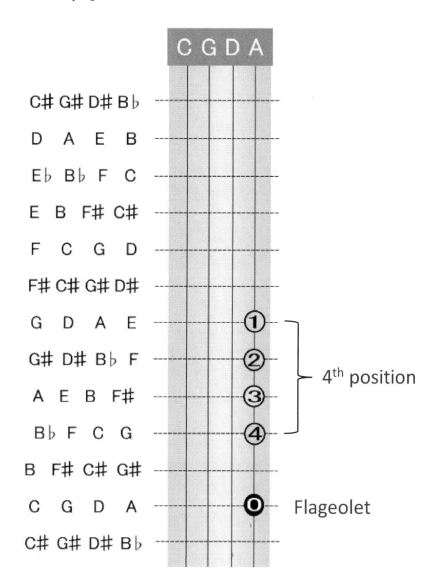

Next, we will further improve your Arpeggio-playing. In this lesson, we will go full range – Arpeggio across all four strings! We start with open strings.

♩=88

M 14.5

[Video 14.5: Arpeggio across four strings]

And now with the left hand involved.

E 14.6

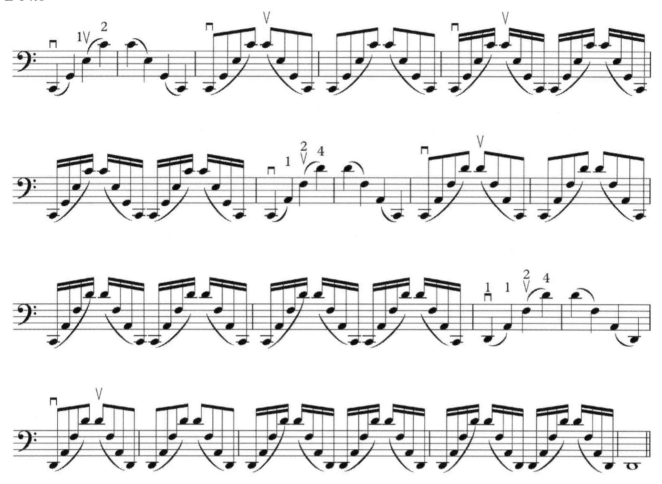

[Video 14.6: Arpeggio across four strings with left hand]

We will practise Arpeggios further with the help of an etude by F.A. Kummer. Remember, his name means "sorrow" or "grief" in English …

♩=80

M 14.7

20

[Video 14.7a: Etude No.90 by F.A. Kummer]
[Video 14.7b: Etude No.90 by F.A. Kummer accompaniment]

Next, we have prepared two preparatory exercises for the second half of the Prelude by Bach.

♩=60

M 14.8

[Video 14.8: Bach exercise No.2]

M 14.9

[Video 14.9: Bach exercise No.3]

And now the second half of the Prelude.

[Video 14.10: Bach Prelude Second Half]

As in the previous lesson, some help to practise.

♩=60

M 14.11

[Video 14.11: Bach exercise No.4]

And finally, an exercise for the execution of the last chord – and we are done!

♩=76

M 14.12

[Video 14.12: Bach exercise No.5]

Prelude

J.S.Bach

Summary of Lesson 14:
- 5th position exercise (including flageolet technique)
- Arpeggio across four strings
- Etude by F.A. Kummer
- Preparatory exercises to the Prelude by Bach
- Second half of the Prelude by Bach

Lesson 15
Time for Romance in Your Life

As you will have noticed, when playing Baroque music, we hardly ever get to rest. Baroque music seems always to be on the move, no matter if played fast or slowly. While this might have something to do with the composers themselves (at more than 1000 pieces, some of them lasting hours, can you imagine Bach ever resting?), it might also be attributed to the bow that was used. A Baroque style bow is bent upwards, and its stick is balanced to the middle, the nut being lighter than that of the modern bow. While quite handy when playing fast moving patterns, there is one thing it can't do – sustain a note, or even do a crescendo on a long note towards the tip.

When the French bow maker François Tourte (1747-1835) introduced his newly designed bow at the end of the 18th century, it was a revolution. By using more wood and giving the player the chance to adjust the tension of the hairs with the help of a screw, it was suddenly possible to sustain longer notes, raising the volume significantly. Beethoven was one of the first composers to realize the potential of the new bow, creating his dynamic accordingly. Thanks to the genius of Tourte, we are now able to play for large audiences.

With longer notes and phrases possible, the development of the vibrato became important. And here the cello suddenly stepped up. Composers such as Schumann, Mendelssohn and Saint-Saëns realized the singing voice (called "Cantilene") of the cello and made ample use of it in their pieces. Never mind the Dvořák Concerto. Or take the music by Schubert, or Brahms, or … Well, back to the lesson. This time, we will practise sustained notes and long phrases. Finally, you will get to play one of the most beautiful pieces of music ever written!

Besides, we will learn the 6th position, thus venturing further and further upwards. In the process, to keep our music writing neat, we will introduce the Tenor-clef.

Ready? Let's go!

First, start with open strings. Try to do an even crescendo towards the tip, and an even diminuendo towards the frog.

♩=84

E 15.1

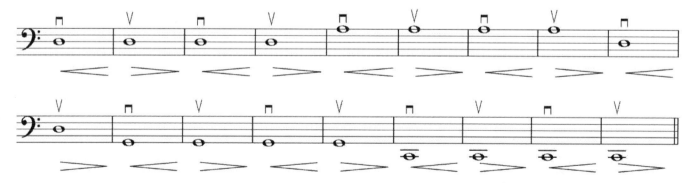

[Video 15.1: Inverted cresc./diminuendi]

Next, use the left hand. Try to follow the crescendo/diminuendi with vibrato – intensify towards the tip, and relax towards the frog.

E 15.2

[Video 15.2: Inverted cresc./diminuendi with vibrato D-string]
And on the A-string:
E15.3

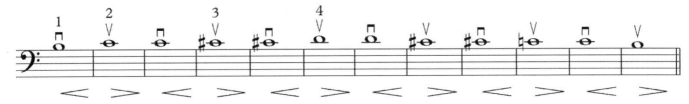

[Video 15.3: Inverted cresc./diminuendi with vibrato A-string]

Next, let's augment this pattern. Again, adjust your vibrato to the dynamics – intensify with crescendo, stay intense in the forte-bar, and relax with diminuendo.

E 15.4

[Video 15.4: Three bar phrase D-string]
Again, on the A-string:

E 15.5

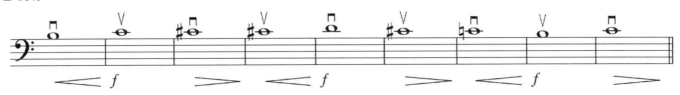

[Video 15.5: Three bar phrase A-string]

Whatever piece we play, the phrasing almost never fits our up- and down-bowing. Thus it is very important for your music not to get stuck in a downbow/upbow pattern.
Before introducing the 6th position, we need the Tenor-clef. The Tenor-clef is a part of the c-clef family. It is basically just an ornament pointing to where the C' goes. By the way, the Bass-clef points to the f, and thus is also called f-clef. In music writing, Bass-clef and Tenor-clef are exactly a fifth apart. Just think one string up, and you should get it!

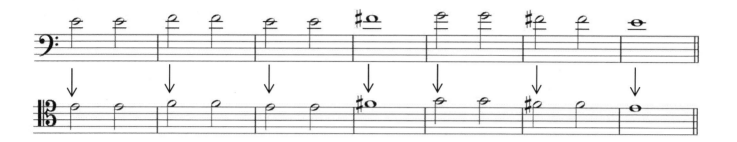

Next, it's time for the 6th position.
First of all, take a look at the 6th position in a graph:

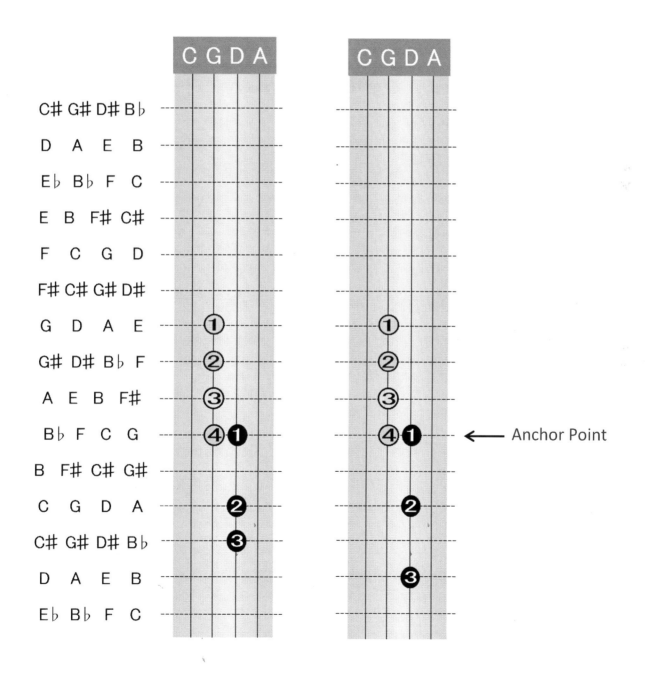

Now let's play.

♩=72

M 15.6

[Video 15.6: 6th position A-string, basic pattern]

Next, the raised version of the 6th position:

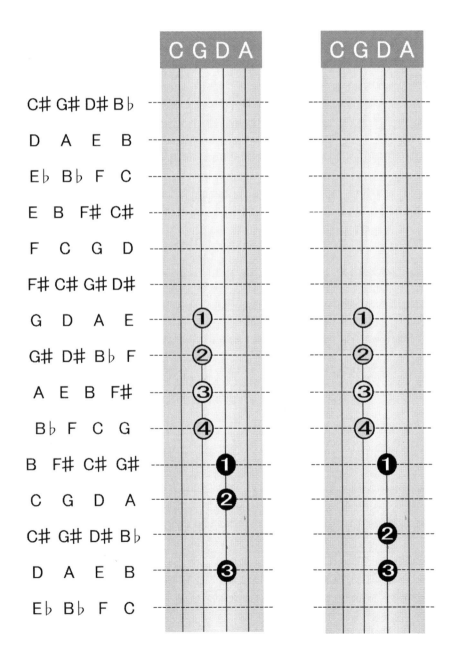

30

M 15.7

[Video 15.7: 6th position A-string, raised pattern]

And on the D-string (for learning purposes, still in the Tenor-clef!)
M 15.8

[Video 15.8: 6th position D-string]

Also the raised version:
M 15.9

[Video 15.9: 6th position D-string, raised pattern]

The scales for this lesson, Bb-Major and B-Major, are rather tricky.

♩=56

M 15.10

[Video 15.10: Bb-Major scale]

M 15.11

[Video 15.11: B-Major scale]

Don't be hasty; watch your intonation and your sound!

Also practise these scales with cresc./diminuendo:

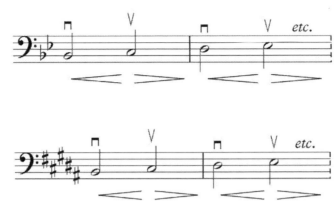

The Etude for this lesson was written by the French cellist Jean-Marie Raoul (1766-1837), who wrote one of the first methods for the cello.

♩=88

M 15.12

[Video 15.12: Etude No.17 by J.M. Raoul]

The piece we chose for this lesson is one of the finest examples of how to produce a singing voice on the cello. In the famous "Vocalise" by Sergei Rachmaninov (1873-1943), there is one seemingly endless phrase going from the beginning to the end of the first half, and then from the beginning of the second half up to the coda. The sound of your instrument must continue throughout these phrases, not to be interrupted by the left hand. Are you up to the challenge?
First, you need to learn to soften your shifts. Imagine your fingerboard being soaked in melted butter (or olive oil for vegetarians!) and produce the finest legato possible.

♩=96

M 15.13

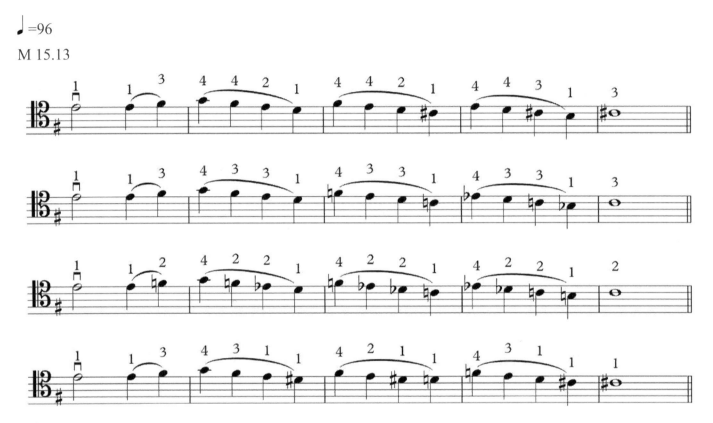

[Video 15.13: Legato shift downwards]

M 15.14

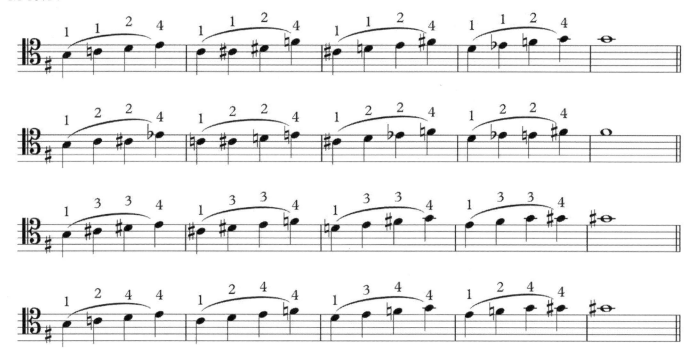

[Video 15.13: Legato shift upwards]

Finally, here is the "Vocalise"!

Sergei Rachmaninov
1873 - 1943

♪=94
M 15.14

[Video 15.14: Vocalise by Rachmaninov]

N.B.: This version of the "Vocalise" is slightly changed from the original concerning the repeats and the ending. If you aim to perform it in public, please purchase the original sheet music.

Summary of Lesson 15:

- Inverted cresc./dim. exercises, phrasing exercises
- 6th position
- Bb-major scale
- B-major scale
- Etude by Raoul
- "Vocalise" exercise
- "Vocalise" by S. Rachmaninov

Lesson 16
Reaching Base Camp

As we observed in the first book of 24 lessons, the fingerboard of the cello is quite long compared to the violin or viola. Sometimes, it feels a little humiliating to observe how seemingly easy it is for the violinists to reach the upper positions. And they are back in first position in no time at all! For us cellists, it is not so easy. Of course, we have much less way to travel than a double-bass player. But still, in order to cover all positions, we need to train thoroughly. Once you are up there, it's easy to get lost!

By now, you have caught a glimpse of the higher positions. That is all well, but to climb even higher (and eventually, to reach the 'heights of the eternal rosin', as a famous cellist put it), we need to organize our ascent. Let's stick with the image of mountain climbing for now. In order to reach the top successfully, it is useful to have a base camp some way up. A base camp should be rather easily accessible from below. From the base camp onwards, serious climbing starts.

Our base camp is the 7th position. The 7th position is located exactly in the geometrical middle of the string. As you know from the previous lesson, it is here where the main flageolet is located. That makes the 7th position easy to find either from below or from the top, thus facilitating both ascent and descent. In short, it is the perfect spot for our base camp!

First, here is a graph to where the base is located:

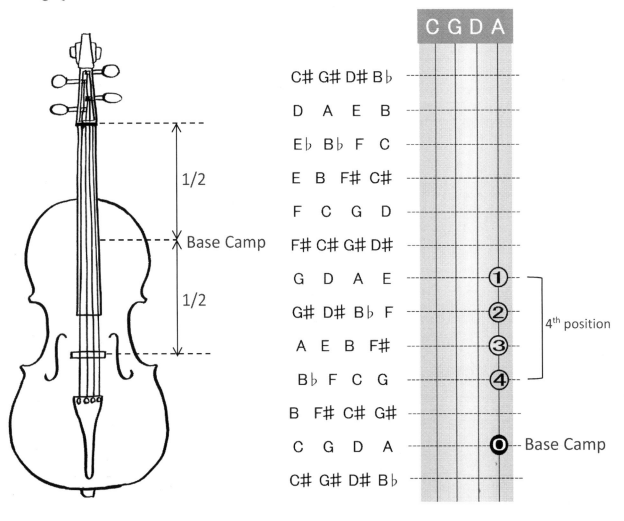

Now let's see if you can find it:

♩=76

M 16.1

[Video 16.1: Finding the "Base Camp"]

It's not difficult to find our base camp, is it? Well, that's the idea. The base camp will play an important role later, when we learn to use the thumb. For now, try to get used to accessing the 7th position from below. Before introducing the 7th position in depth, let's practise some other forms of access.

M 16.2

[Video 16.2: Accessing the "Base Camp"]

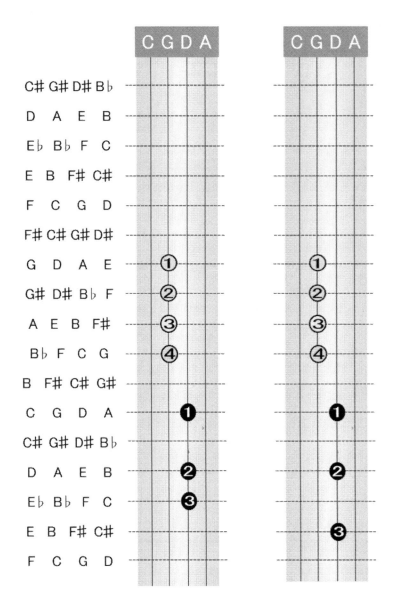

Notice that the angle of the left hand changes quite a lot when accessing the 7th position. Make sure to adjust the wrist, too. The wrist must not rest on the cello, but there should always be a little air between wrist and wood.

Now, let's practise the 7th position.
M 16.3

[Video 16.3: 7th position]

40

Important Note

When accessing the 7th position (or passing through), it is a safe and easy option to use the flageolet. However, once you are settled, you should push the string down to the fingerboard as with any other note. Otherwise, the note will always acoustically stand out, because you can't vibrate. Ultimately, it's up to each player's good taste to decide how much to use the flageolet. In our opinion, using it too much makes for a rather cold and technical playing style.

Here is the longest scale you have practised so far!

♩=84

M 16.4

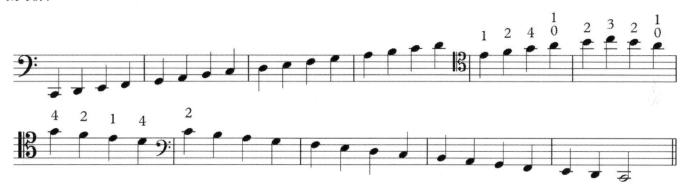

[Video 16.4: C-Major 3 octaves]
Practise also with legato.
M 16.4b

The 7th position is the last position before the thumb comes into play. Whenever we need to get down immediately, the 7th position is used. However, since the hand moves up the fingerboard, the angle is quite different. Let's focus on the position of the thumb. **Before practicing the next exercise, watch the video carefully!**

♩=68

M 16.5

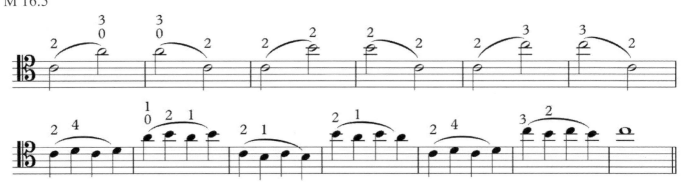

[Video 16.5: Shifting between 1st and 7th position]

It's very important to bridge this rather huge distance. The thumb provides security and orientation to the left hand. It is a common mistake to lift the thumb when shifting into the 7th position. It's like jumping in the dark – you might be lucky to hit the spot, especially when playing at home in your cosy practise study, but very likely your luck will run out when you play with or for other people. Believe us; whenever you are on stage, you need a safe system. By the way, this doesn't affect the dramatic aspects of your playing at all. It's like a good tightrope walker in the circus – it might look dangerous, but professional artists usually know what they are doing! Next, let's practise to access the 7th position from the 4th position.

M 16.6

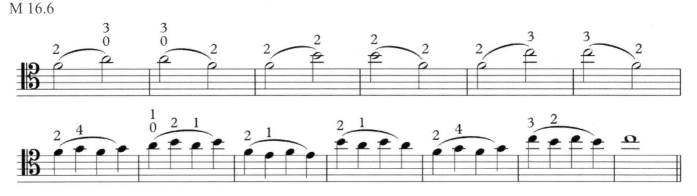

[Video 16.6: Shifting between 4th and 7th position]

Now it's time for our etude. We will once again refer to Mr. Kummer, this time it's his No.86.

♪ =60

M 16.7

[Video 16.7a: Kummer Etude No.86]
[Video 16.7b: Kummer Etude No.86 2nd cello]

Important Note

When exercising shifts, make sure to adjust the speed of your shifting to the general pace of the music. There is no need to rush when playing slowly. Stay relaxed; don't jerk your left hand. This is important, because when playing a faster piece, you will be used to a complete frameset of movements that you can accelerate or slow down if needed.

You will presumably know the piece for this lesson very well – the famous English melody Greensleeves. Since you know the piece very well (or, at least, you will know it well shortly!), we challenge you to play a difficult version. When the melody appears one octave higher, you should not compromise on the quality of your playing: keep an eye and an ear on intonation, sound, vibrato and phrasing!

Green sleeves

♩=98

M 16.8

[Video 16.8a: Greensleeves]
[Video 16.8b: Greensleeves 2nd cello]

Summary of Lesson 16:
- Introduction of the 7th position, finding "base camp"
- C-major scale across 3 octaves
- Shifting to the 7th position from 1st and 4th positions
- Etude by Kummer
- Greensleeves

Lesson 17
Chopping Away

As an eager student, you will surely remember lesson No.5 in the first volume of this method. Back then we learned how to improve the style of your playing by applying a bowing called *portato* (do we hear the penny drop?). Briefly, we explained that *portato* is a bowing style somewhat between *legato* and *staccato*. Well, by now we are sure you do a nice *legato*, which we will cultivate further in the next lesson. In this lesson, we will introduce the technique of *staccato*. *Staccato* (Italian for "divided") means that you play several notes on one bow, yet make a clear distinction between single notes. The bow almost comes to a complete stop, thus making this technique rather difficult in faster tempos.

Both *staccato* and *spiccato* (to play bouncing notes) are a dreaded pair of bowing styles with many a cellist. However, it all comes down to the right technique. When playing *staccato*, raise your elbow a bit, but make sure to keep your right shoulder and upper arm relaxed. The nitty gritty work, i.e. the subdivision of the strokes, is done by the right hand and fingers.

♩=88

M 17.1

[Video 17.1: Staccato basics]

Reversed or down-bow *staccato* is even trickier. Again, try to relax your upper right arm and shoulder!
M 17.2

[Video 17.2: Down-bow Staccato]

Next, we will practise *staccato* on all four strings. Note how stubborn the C-string behaves. It is really hard to get a good sound down there!

M 17.3

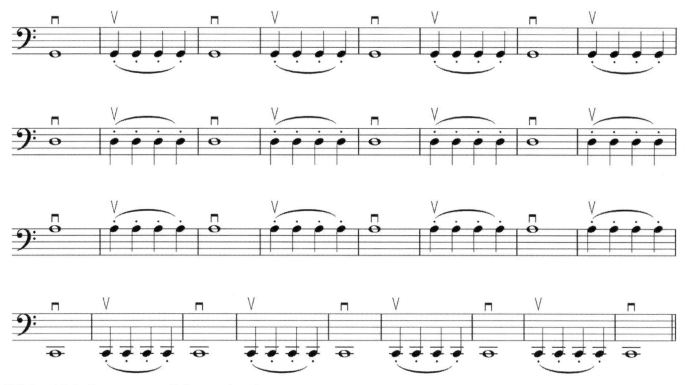

[Video 17.3: Staccato on all four strings]

When we involve the left hand, coordination is most important. Try to synchronize the placement of the fingers of the left hand exactly in accordance to the movement of the bow.

♩=80

M 17.4

[Video 17.4: Staccato with left hand involved]

As with any playing style, we need to speed things up a bit. Don't despair if you can't do it perfectly right now. Focus on not losing a good articulation!

♩=80
M 17.5a

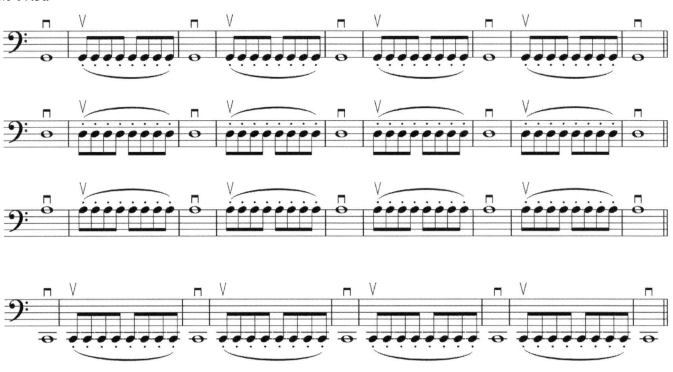

[Video 17.5a: Fast Staccato]

The ultimate challenge (and the domain of the famous violinist Jascha Haifetz!) is a fast down-bow *staccato*. When possible, it is avoided within a piece. However, try to practise it thoroughly. In the course, you will definitely feel an improvement of your up-bow *staccato* as well.

M 17.5b

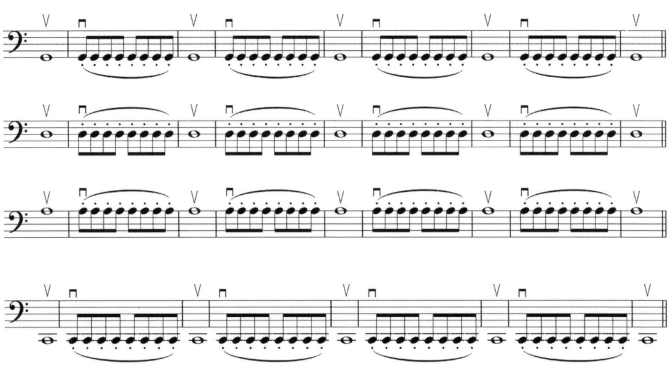

[Video 17.5b: Fast Down-bow Staccato]

Scales are a great way to practise any type of bowing. Try to start the C-major scale both down-bow and up-bow!

M 17.6

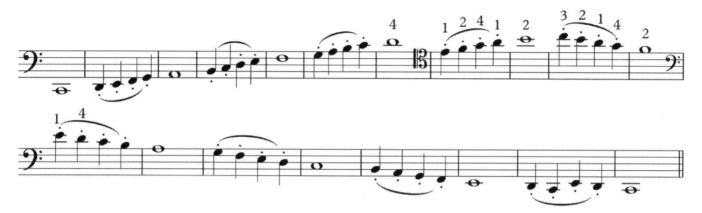

[Video 17.6a: C-Major scale with Staccato – Down-bow]
[Video 17.6b: C-Major scale with Staccato – Up-bow]

Sebastian Lee wouldn't be our etude-guru if he didn't provide a nice piece to apply staccato. Here is his No.25.

[Video 17.7: S. Lee No.25]

Enough bowing exercises for now, don't you think? Let's put the bow away for now. Very few people ever think about how to produce a nice pizzicato. Yet, it is one of the strong points of the cello. In opera arias or any other accompaniment, it gives the soloist their bass notes, while controlling the timing and the tempo. In chamber music, it can provide any effect from harp-like chords (like in the second movement of the String Quintet in C-major by Schubert) or rain drops (like in the fourth movement of the Piano Quintet by Dvořàk). In some pieces, it can be challengingly fast (like in the second movement of the String Quartet by Debussy) or slow and antagonizing (like the slow chords at the end of "Transfigured Night" by Schönberg.)

The pizzicato is usually executed by the middle finger of the right hand for single notes, and with the thumb when playing chords (with notable exceptions to this rule!). Try to strike the string between the middle and the lower end of the fingerboard. Make sure to use the soft part at the tip of your middle finger. It helps to trim your fingernails first …

M 17.8

[Video 17.8: Pizzicato Demonstration]

When placing the fingers of the left hand, make sure to hold the string down well for a longer sound.

♩=76

M 17.9

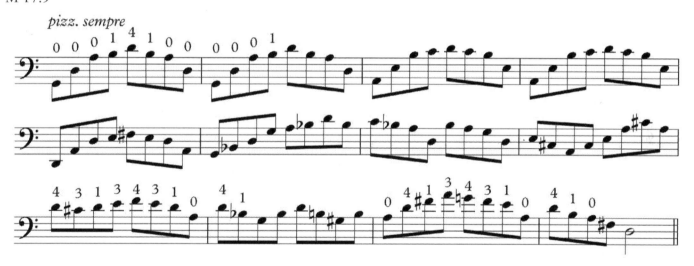

[Video 17.9: Pizzicato Exercise]

The piece for this lesson is a so called *Siciliano* or *Siciliana* (*Sicilienne* in French). A *Siciliano* is a dance, almost always written in 6/8 measure, which is characterized by its rhythm:

In this lesson, we will introduce the famous *Sicilienne* by Gabriel Fauré. Both elegant and stylish, it is one of the pieces where cellists can really enjoy the sound of their instrument! Pay attention to get the pizzicato bits right. Don't compromise on the quality of sound!

51

[Video 17.10: "Sicilienne" by G. Fauré]

Let's have a look at bar 26. Take enough time for the shift, don't move the bow before the left hand is safely in place!

♩=76

M 17.11

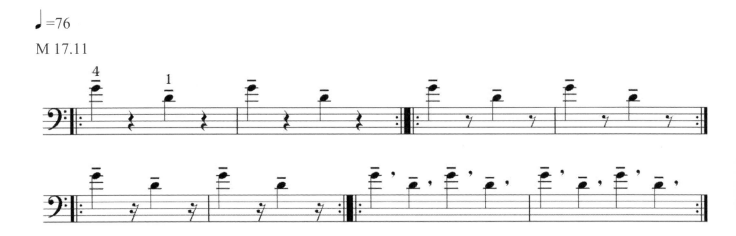

[Video 17.11: Shift exercise for "Sicilienne" by G. Fauré]

Summary of Lesson 17:
- Introduction of the staccato technique
- Staccato exercises both up- and dow-bow
- Staccato with the left hand involved
- Etude by Lee
- Pizzicato technique, basics
- "Sicilienne" by Gabriel Fauré

Lesson 18
Slithering Along

Don't you sometimes wake up in the middle of the night feeling that you have to do something about your *legato*? Just kidding, but in this lesson we will strive to improve your legato skills across strings. As we mentioned on various occasions, being flexible is most important when playing together with others.

There are many examples of famous composers who wrote fantastic music – yet obviously didn't know much about string instruments. Brahms comes to mind, with his famous legato-tremolo in the first movement of his F-major Sonata op.99. Or think of the Finale of the Pastorale Symphony by Beethoven. Even the first movement of the "Spring" by Vivaldi is not easy – many cellists have a hard time keeping the tempo when playing legato across strings. In short – to prepare you for the various challenges that lie ahead, in this lesson we will try to improve your agility across two strings.

First, let's start slowly, getting gradually faster. In the end, when playing sixteenth, the right wrist should perform a small wave-like motion. Elbow, upper arm and shoulder should stay relaxed.

♩=72

M 18.1a

[Video 18.1a: Legato across strings]

And the same from above.

M 18.1b

[Video 18.1b: Legato across strings from above]

Next, let's get the left hand involved. Take care to compromise neither on intonation nor sound quality.

M 18.2

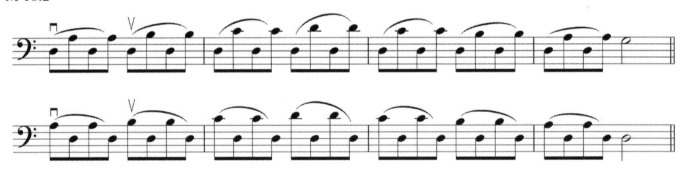

[Video 18.2: Legato across strings with left hand]

Involving all strings is a little tricky at first. You will notice that you have to apply more pressure on the lower strings, while relieving the bow when you go up. Practise in three tempos:

♩=60, 82, 104

M 18.3

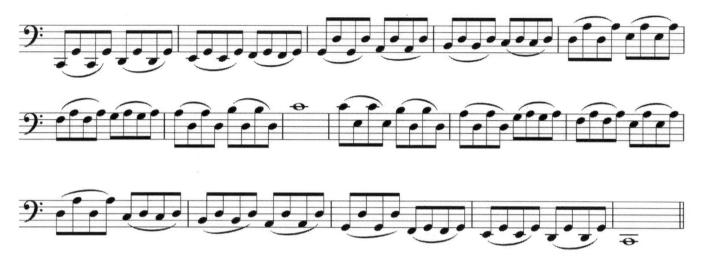

[Video 18.3: C-Major scale legato across strings]

Friedrich Dotzauer is infamous for applying one pattern in each of his etudes, usually sticking to this pattern until the bitter end. That's why most cellists utter his name always together with a sigh …

Yet in this lesson, we want to improve your stamina – if you make it to the end of the etude without feeling too tired, you got the bowing right! So, here is Dotzauer's Etude No.39.

[Video 18.4: Dotzauer Etude No.39 legato across strings]

Next, we have one more exercise. To make sure your left hand is completely at home throughout positions 5-7, we have added this position exercise by Joseph Werner.

♩=84

M 18.5

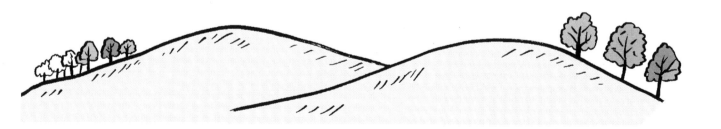

[Video 18.5: Werner Position exercise]

The piece for this lesson was written by the famous Russian composer Alexander Glazunov (1865-1936). His Sérénade Espagnole op.20/2 is one of the nicest short pieces for cello and orchestra. It was written in 1888, a time when Glazunov started to be recognized as a serious composer. Of course, the Sérénade Espagnole is equally charming with piano accompaniment!

Before starting, let's have a look at the grace notes. Slashed grace notes are to be played on the beat.

61

[Video 18.6: "Sérénade Espagnole" by A. Glazunov]

Summary of Lesson 18:

- Legato across two strings, open strings, both from below and from above
- Legato across two strings with the left hand involved
- Legato variation of the C-major scale
- Etude by F. Dotzauer
- Position exercise by J. Werner
- "Sérénade Espagnole" by Alexander Glazunov

Alexander Glazunov
1865 - 1936

Lesson 19
Scaling the Heights

By now, you should have settled comfortably in your base camp. If you are not sure what we are talking about, better go back to lesson 16 for a moment. For this lesson, it is essential that you are absolutely feeling safe from positions 1 to 7. If climbing a hill is too much for you, you can't very well scale a mountain, can you?

But rest assured, we are there to help you on your way up. There is no need to panic: remember that our Base Camp Position also serves as a safety net. Even if you get lost higher up, you can always return there. Neat, isn't it? So, let's go. First, we must try to get the thumb up and in position. The thumb is always placed on two strings at once. Have a look at the video of how to place the thumb. Remember to keep both your left wrist and hand in a natural position.

[Video D 19.1: Placing of the thumb]

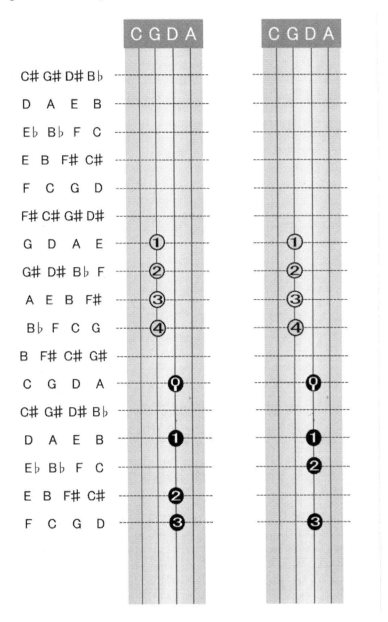

The thumb is indicated with this symbol:

Now, feel your way up, by accessing base camp first, and then going up.

♩=76

M 19.1

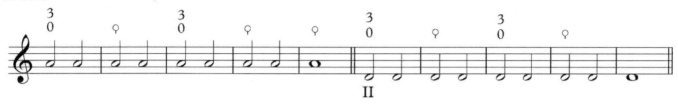

[Video 19.1: Getting the thumb into position]

Now let's place the other fingers, too.

M 19.2

[Video 19.2: First steps in the thumb position]

Next, place the fingers also on the D-string.

M 19.3

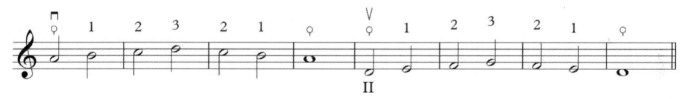

[Video 19.3: Thumb position A-string and D-string]

With these notes, you are able to play the Dorian scale. Do you remember the Dorian scale from the first volume?

M 19.4

[Video 19.4: Dorian scale thumb position]

Next, we move the second finger a half step up.

M 19.5

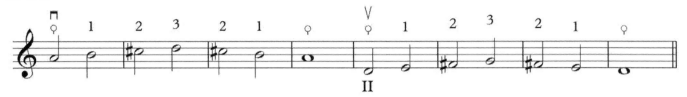

[Video 19.5: Thumb position variation A-string and D-string]

Before you know it, the Dorian scale turns into a Major scale.

M 19.6

[Video 19.6: D-Major scale thumb position]

Next, we have a little etude written by Martin Stanzeleit for you. Don't forget to check your sound! When the left hand moves up on the fingerboard, the contact point of the bow should be adjusted accordingly – move a few millimetres towards the bridge (not too much – if you hear a brittle, husky sound, you have obviously moved too far!).

♩=76

M 19.7

[Video 19.7a: Etude in the thumb position M. Stanzeleit]
[Video 19.7b: Etude in the thumb position M. Stanzeleit 2nd cello]

Next, we want you to practise a Scherzando by Friedrich Kummer, a perfect piece to become even more familiar with the thumb position.

♪ =84

M 19.8

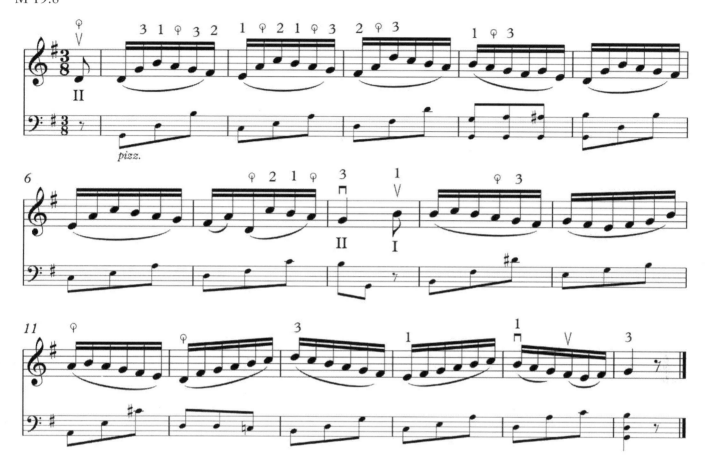

[Video 19.8a: Scherzando in the thumb position by F. Kummer]
[Video 19.8b: Scherzando in the thumb position by F. Kummer 2nd cello]

Finally our piece for this lesson – here is "The Swan" by Camille Saint-Saëns. The crown jewel of all short pieces ever written for the cello, there is hardly an educated person in the world who hasn't heard this wonderful melody. Before you can enjoy playing this wonderful music, let's practise two shifts that need special attention.

♩ =76

M 19.9

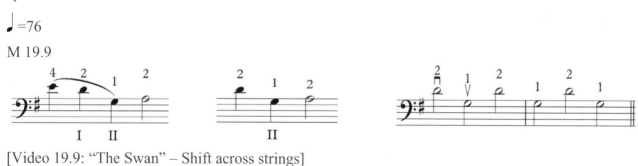

[Video 19.9: "The Swan" – Shift across strings]

M 19.10

[Video 19.10: "The Swan" – Shift exercise]

M 19.11

[Video 19.11: "The Swan" by C. Saint-Saëns]

Summary of Lesson 19:
- Introduction of the thumb position
- Placing the thumb
- Thumb position exercise and Dorian scale
- Thumb position exercise variation and D-major scale
- Etude by M. Stanzeleit
- Etude by F. Kummer
- "The Swan" by C. Saint-Saëns

Camille Saint-Saëns
1835-1921

Lesson 20
Fast and Furious

Do you remember? In the first part of 24 lessons, we tried to speed up your playing. Back then, it took quite an effort, didn't it? By now you are an advanced player, thus you need to be able to play both fast and strong. Playing quick strokes without losing both sound and articulation is not so easy, but it is the basic way of handling faster pieces. The bowing in question is called *Detaché*, which is actually French meaning "single", "separated". Interestingly, with some newer bowing styles, terms and definitions moved from Italian to French. As you will remember from lesson 15, the modern bow ("modern" in this context meaning only a little over 200 years old …) was invented in France, and with it some of the playing styles that hadn't been possible before.

When playing the following exercise, make sure that each note is clear! Remember to use the space between balance point (S) and middle (M) of the bow. Check the video to make sure you got the right spot.

[Video 20.1: Detached bowing exercise on the D-string]

Next, let's try the same on the A-string.

M 20.2

[Video 20.2: Detached bowing exercise on the A-string]

The more fingers of the left hand get involved, the more difficult it gets. If you struggle to coordinate right and left hand, remember to put a slight accent at the beginning of each group of notes.

♩=96

M 20.3

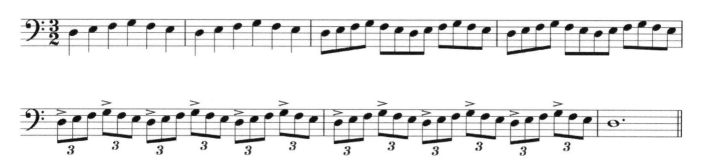

[Video 20.3: Detached bowing exercise on the D-string involving the fourth finger]

And the same on the A-string.

M 20.4

[Video 20.4: Detached bowing exercise on the A-string involving the fourth finger]

Next, we will use this bowing technique to practise the G-Major scale. There are three patterns, easy, medium and difficult.

♩=96

M 20.5a

[Video 20.5a: G-Major scale easy pattern]

M 20.5b

[Video 20.5b: G-Major scale medium pattern]

M 20.5c

[Video 20.5c: G-Major scale difficult pattern]

The last one isn't so easy, is it? Again, put a little accent on each group of four notes to organize the pattern.

Next, we will give your right hand a chance to relax a bit. Let's try the D-Major scale from the first position up to the basic thumb position.

♩=76

M 20.6

[Video 20.6: D-Major scale up to the basic thumb position]

Are you rested and ready? Then we won't keep you waiting any longer. The etude for this lesson is an exercise in detached bowing by Sebastian Lee.

Sebastian Lee
1805 - 1887

73

74

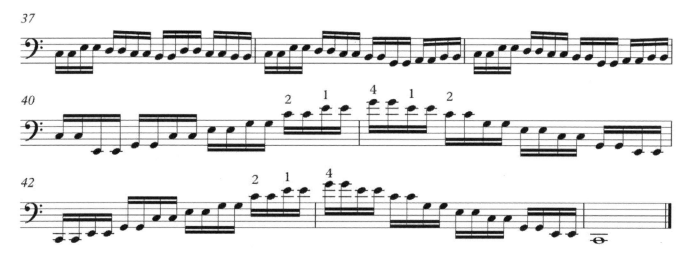

[Video 20.7: Exercise in Detached Bowing by S. Lee]

The piece for this lesson is the gorgeous "Song Without Words" opus 109 by Felix Mendelssohn-Bartholdy. The version for this lesson is slightly modified; we strongly recommend that you purchase the sheet music of the original edition!

Felix Mendelssohn-Bartholdy
1809 - 1847

M 20.8
♩=66

Andante con moto

[Video 20.8: "Song Without Words" by Mendelssohn]

Summary of Lesson 20:
- Detaché exercise on the D-string
- Detaché exercise on the A-string
- Advanced left hand detaché exercise on the D-string
- Advanced left hand detaché exercise on the A-string
- D-major scale from first through to thumb position
- Etude by S. Lee
- "Song Without Words" by F. Mendelssohn-Bartholdy

Ten Commandments of Practicing

1. Plan ahead before you start practicing
   - what do you want to achieve?

2. How much time do you allot for what?

3. Be clear about your goals - but be
   prepared to call it a day and continue
   in your next session

4. Don't set unrealistic goals that will
   only leave you frustrated. Take one
   step at a time.

5. Use a metronome to measure your
   progress - but finish your practice
   session without

6. If something doesn't seem to work, take
   a step back. Play slower, check your
   basic playing style

7. Never forget to check your intonation

8. Never forget the quality of your sound

9. Try to enjoy your time with the cello
   and keep your body relaxed

10. Have a break once in a while!

Lesson 21
Time for Sports

Whenever you talk to a cellist, you will encounter a certain disinclination of the bowing technique called *spiccato*. Most amateur cellists hate it – but that isn't fair. You can learn to play *spiccato* exactly as you can learn any other technique on the cello. Admittedly, it is a sporty way of bowing, and you should be willing to focus on the physical aspect of playing. But we promise, once you have mastered the basics of the *spiccato*, it's a lot of fun! It is usually required in light and quick pieces. So, no need to be grumpy!

A good *spiccato* is a combination between vertical and horizontal bowing. Try to get a feeling for bouncing your bow vertically, as if jumping on a trampoline. It doesn't produce a pitched sound at all, but we are doing it to get the motion right. After that, we will combine it with broader sideway strokes and thus produce a bouncing sound that has a lot of potential for musical expression.

[Video D 21.1: Spiccato technique]

One more thing before you get going: It takes some stamina to learn a good *spiccato*. Most players think "I will never be able to do it!" and give up immediately. What a big mistake! Almost nobody is born to play the cello perfectly, and that includes many different styles of bowing. The author of this method struggled many years to master the *spiccato* perfectly. Then, one day, he woke up – and suddenly it was there! Think like an athlete and never give up.

Note that in the first exercise, the sixteenth notes are neither up- or down-bow. Just let your bow drop onto the string and feel it bouncing up again, like a basketball. Don't hold the bow too tight.

♩=76

M 21.1

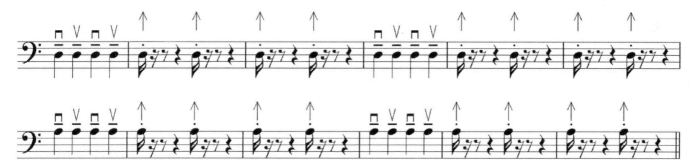

[Video 21.1: Bouncing Spiccato Exercise]

In the next exercise, we will combine vertical and horizontal bowing. Don't give up on the bouncing part – if not sure, go back to the exercise above. Also, take your time! You really need to train your right hand. Repeat the next exercise several times.

♩=108

M 21.2

[Video 21.2: Spiccato Exercise Open Strings]

Next, we will involve the left hand.

M 21.3

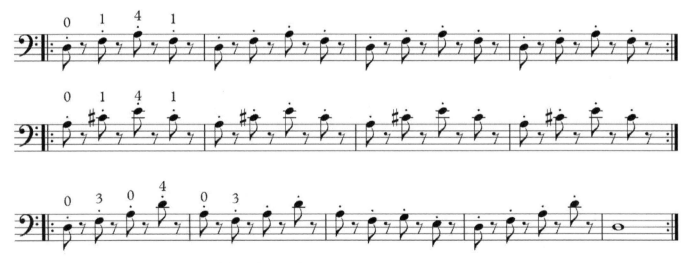

[Video 21.3: Spiccato Exercise With Left Hand]

Next, try to achieve a regular bouncing motion.

♩=108

M 21.4

[Video 21.4: Regular Spiccato Exercise Open Strings]

Then, we will combine two strings. Before you know it, the left hand will be involved, too!

M 21.5

[Video 21.5: Regular Spiccato Exercise Two Strings Combined]

Next, we do the same on the G- and D-strings.

M 21.6

[Video 21.6: Regular Spiccato Exercise G- and D-String]

Finally, we get close to the real thing. No more repeated notes! Again, make sure to keep the bow bouncing.

♩=108

M 21.7

[Video 21.7: Flexible Spiccato Exercise]

Now, it's time to try a scale in this way!
M 21.8

[Video 21.8: G-Major Scale Spiccato Version]

We are not done yet … The etude for this lesson, No.35 by Friedrich Kummer, requires a good handling of the spiccato technique.

♩=60

M 21.9

[Video 21.9: Etude No.35 by F. Kummer]

Finally, we are done. Enough *spiccato* for now! Let's move on to "Salut d'Amour" by Edward Elgar. There is hardly a more charming melody than in this piece. One more reason to make it a part of your repertoire!

♩=84
M 21.10

Allegretto

2

p dolce legatissimo

84

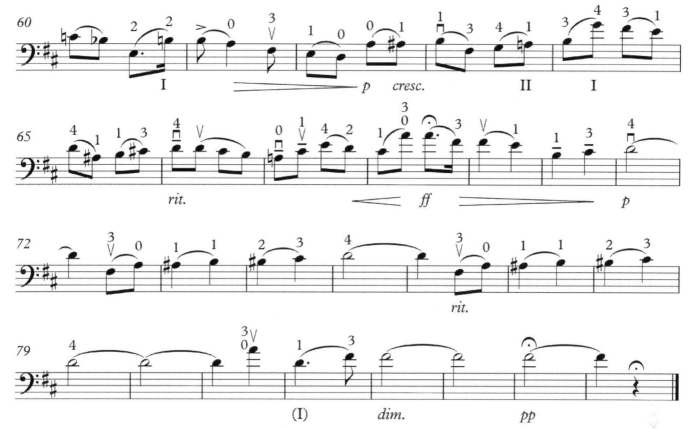

[Video 21.10: "Salut d'Amour" by E. Elgar]

Summary of Lesson 21:

- Basic spiccato exercises
- Spiccato exercises involving the left hand
- Regular spiccato exercise
- Regular spiccato exercise involving the left hand
- G-major scale with spiccato
- Etude by F. Kummer
- "Salut d'Amour" by Edward Elgar

Lesson 22
Elegance and Style

All cellists have a certain pride when it comes to their instrument. Of course, all other instrumentalists have a certain pride, too, but – isn't the cello the most elegant of all? Well, try to argue with a flute or a harp player about this. Take any orchestra of, say, 60 players, and you will have 60 different opinions about which instrument has the best sound, the nicest look, the most appeal, and so on. So, no need to elaborate. Let's stay within the community of cellists, and for us the cello is without doubt the most elegant of all instruments. In this lesson, we will focus on the traditional means of improving elegance and style. Going back to the Baroque era, "elegance" first and foremost meant decorative elements like mordents, trills and the like. To produce a good trill, you need a good articulation in the left hand. To improve the clarity of your left hand, make sure to drop the fingers on the fingerboard. Even when practising without the bow, the notes should be audible.

[Video D 22.1: Left hand articulation]

♩=84

M 22.1

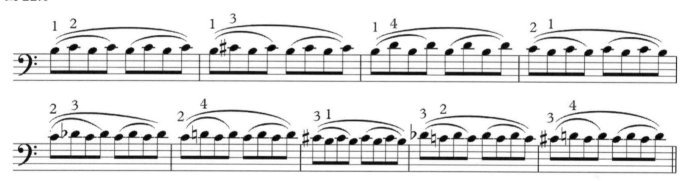

[Video 22.1: Two Finger Exercise]

87

M 22.2

[Video 22.2: Three Finger Exercise]

Advice: You may help the fourth finger by supporting its motion with the back of your hand.
Next, let's practise trills. For a trill to be executed beautifully, it is not important to be fast. Try to focus on clarity and intonation.

M 22.3

[Video 22.3: Trill Exercise]

=84

M 22.4

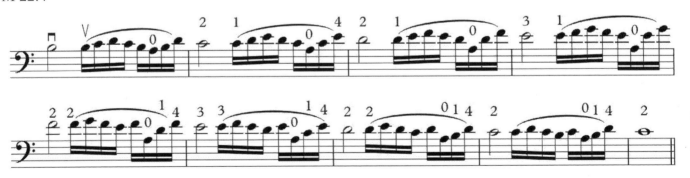

[Video 22.4: Doppelschlag Exercise]

♩=84

M 22.5

[Video 22.5: Mordent Exercise]

Let's advance your thumb position further. Without changing the thumb and third finger position, there are several combinations possible. Note where the half tones and whole tones are – watch your left hand to get it right. In bar 6, the first finger has to literally "cling" to the thumb. It might take a little time to get used to playing this position. Don't forget to check your intonation and sound on the way!

♩=76

M 22.6

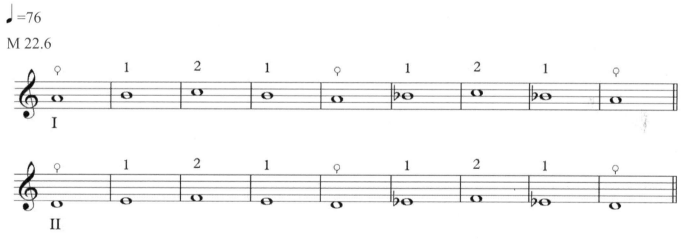

[Video 22.6: Thumb Position B]

M 22.7

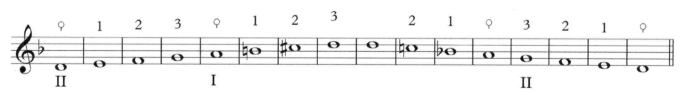

[Video 22.7: D-minor scale/Thumb position version]

M 22.8

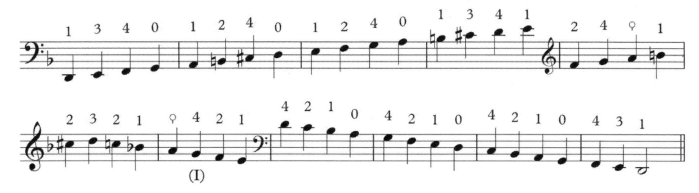

[Video 22.8: D-minor scale/Three octaves]

The etude for this lesson was written by Bernhard Romberg, a German cellist who for some time worked alongside Beethoven in the court orchestra in Bonn. Instead of focussing just on the technical elements of this piece, try to get the character right. The "Tempo di Menuetto" should sound charming and playful!
Etude: "Tempo di menuetto" by Bernhard Romberg

♩=88

M 22.9

[Video 22.9: "Tempo die menuetto" by Bernhard Romberg]

The piece for this lesson was written by the Dutch composer Willem de Fesch. He was slightly younger than Bach and worked first in Antwerpen and later in London. There exists no proof, but he might have known Beethoven's grandfather (Ludwig van Beethoven the Elder, 1712-1773), who was active in the region at the same time. His Sonata in d-minor is both elegant and intense, thus being a perfect fit for this lesson! "Siciliano and Allemand" from the Sonata d-minor by Willem de Fesch (1695-1758)

[Video 22.10: "Siciliano and Allemanda" from the Sonata d-minor by W. de Fesch]

Willem de Fesch
1695 - 1758

Lesson 23
Full Harmony

Do you remember the vibrato lesson in the first volume? How good it felt to have your instrument vibrating, and how you used it to create your vibrato? With double-stops, it is somewhat similar. Double-stops are dreaded by many cellists, because they just never sound perfectly right. Many players frantically move their fingers on both strings involved, determined to find the correct spot – forgetting completely to take care of their sound. Yet the key to perform a good double-stop – and this might come as a surprise – is your bow and thus your right hand. Before even starting to think about intonation, there are three requirements to be met first: The sound of the lower string, the sound of the upper string, and the balance between those two strings. If any of these requirements is not met, it doesn't really matter if your intonation is good or bad – simply because you won't be able to hear it. In short: no sound, no pitch.

But don't worry. With a little patience, you will be able to learn the art of playing double-stops. Just imagine how nice and rewarding it will be at the end of this lesson to be able to play Bach's Sarabande properly. And that is well worth a little effort, don't you think so? Good.

Before starting, it might be a good idea to check the exercises on double stops in the first volume. Because now, we will start at an advanced level.

 =82

M 23.1

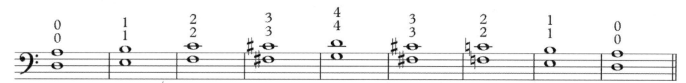

[Video 23.1: Double stops in fifths]

M 23.2

[Video 23.2: Double stops in fifths, A-string]

M 23.3

[Video 23.3: Double stops in fourths]

M 23.4

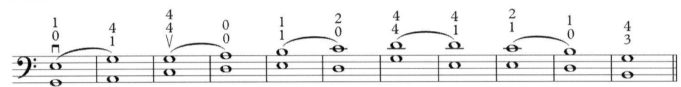

[Video 23.4: Double stops in sixths]

M 23.5

[Video 23.5: Mixed Double stops]

M 23.6

[Video 23.6: Double stops with slurs]

M 23.7

[Video 23.7: Double stops advanced position]

When practising double stops, scales are an unavoidable step. Admittedly rather difficult, we urge you not to change your approach – don't forget to take care of your sound!

♩=82

M 23.8

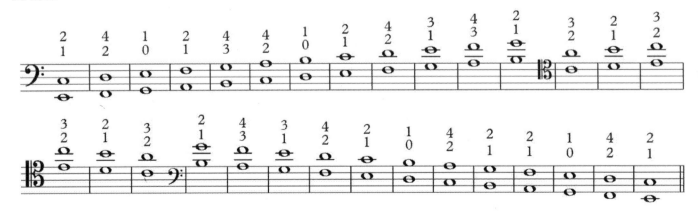

[Video 23.8: C-major scale in sixths]

Next, let's extend your range of the thumb. When using the thumb on the D- and G-strings, there is a risk of losing clarity in sound. Try to match the sound of the A-string as closely as possible.

♩=60

M 23.9

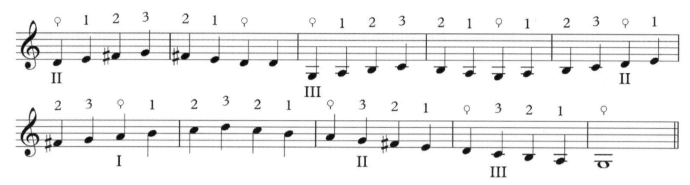

[Video 23.9: Thumb position G-string]

The etude for this lesson is provided by Friedrich Dotzauer. Yes, we know, Dotzauer is probably never going to be your favourite composer, yet he has the function of a good dentist. He is not really popular, you are happy not to meet him too frequently – yet what he does is important, and he does it well.

♩=82

M 23.10

Friedrich Dotzauer

[Video 23.10: Dotzauer No.63]

After suffering through this etude – disentangled your fingers yet? – we will reward you with the Sarabande from the 1st Suite for Cello solo by Johann Sebastian Bach. Wherever possible, try to apply everything you have learned in the exercises and in the etude.

♪ =72

M 23.11

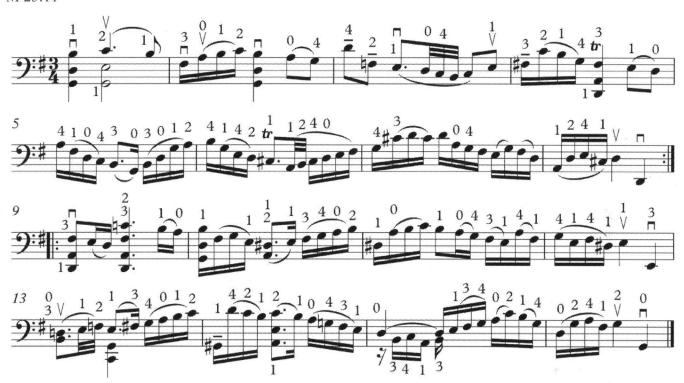

[Video 23.11: Sarabande by Bach]

Summary of Lesson 23:
- Double stops fifths, fourths, sixths, mixed
- Double stops with slurs
- Double stops advanced position
- C-major in sixths
- Thumb exercise on D- and G-string
- Etude No.63 by Friedrich Dotzauer
- Sarabande from the Suite No.1 in G-major by Johann Sebastian Bach

Lesson 24
Roaming the Fingerboard

Congratulations on reaching the last lesson! We presume you have faithfully studied all previous lessons, practised all exercises, watched all videos, and did all the homework given to you. Well done! No matter if you started out as a total beginner or with a little previous experience in playing, by now you should have reached a fairly advanced standard.

Before releasing you into the wild, and to sum up this method of playing, we want to provide you with one of the most important techniques any cellist needs in daily life: shifts. Almost any piece that you will play from now on will require a good shifting technique. Shifts should be part of your music rather than just technical moves. Try to find good examples for shifts and listen how gracefully the masters of the trade connect two notes. One such spot is the little *ritornello* at the end of each variation in Tchaikovsky's "Variations on a Rococo Theme". The shift is performed on the A-string first, later it appears one octave lower on both G- and D-strings.

The goal of this lesson is to give you a good feeling when covering the distance between two notes. Some shifts are performed in a matter-of-fact style, just aiming at the following note. Others are enjoyed thoroughly. Anyway, a shift must not block your music. It should always be part of a phrase, even a tool to develop a phrase.

Let's start with pattern 1 – the fingers used for the bottom and top notes are in rising order (the same order as your hand). Type [a] is better suited for clarity and articulation. Type [b] incorporates a glissando and thus produces a very soft connection.

[Video 24.1a: Pattern 1 type a]

[Video 24.1b: Pattern 1 type b]

M 24.2

I *sempre*

[Video 24.2: Shift technique Pattern 1]

♩=66

M 24.3

I *sempre*

[Video 24.3: Shift exercise Pattern 1 type a/A-string]

M 24.4

II *sempre*

[Video 24.4: Shift exercise Pattern 1 type a/D-string]

M 24.5

I *sempre*

[Video 24.5: Shift exercise Pattern 1 type b/A-string]

M 24.6

[Video 24.6: Shift exercise Pattern 1 type b/D-string]

Pattern 2 is a shift where both bottom and top notes are played with the same finger.

M 24.7

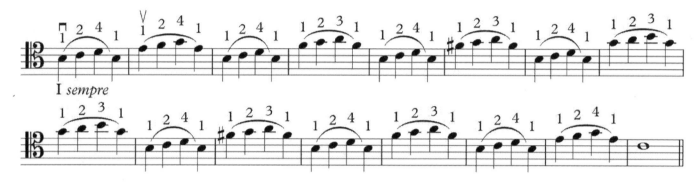

[Video 24.7: Pattern 2 – Shift exercise with same finger/A-string]

M 24.8

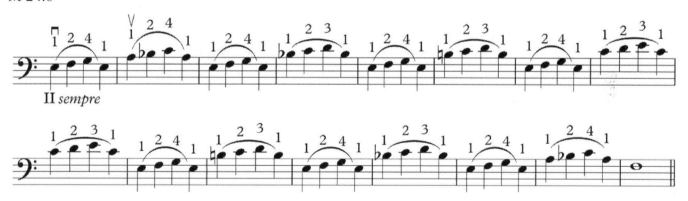

[Video 24.8: Pattern 2 – Shift exercise with same finger/D-string]

Pattern 3 is a shifting technique used when bottom and top notes demand a reverse fingering. Here, without stopping, a lower finger takes the place of the previous one and slides up.

M 24.9

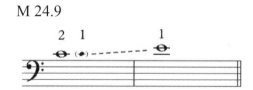

[Video 24.9: Pattern 3 – Shift with lower finger]

M 24.10

I *sempre*

[Video 24.10: Pattern 2 – Basic shift technique]

♩=76

M 24.11

I *sempre*

[Video 24.11: Pattern 3 – Shift with lower finger, A-string]

M 24.12

II *sempre*

[Video 24.12: Pattern 3 – Shift with lower finger, D-string]

M 24.13

I *sempre*

[Video 24.13: Shift with lower finger, pattern 2/A-string]

M 24.14

II *sempre*

[Video 24.14: Shift with lower finger, pattern 2/D-string]

Finally, we want to further improve the use of the thumb. Until now, the thumb remained fixed in one position. In this lesson, we want to move the thumb to a different position. Your hand should move like an elevator, with the thumb deciding which "floor" you are going to stop at.

♩=60

M 24.15

[Video 24.15: Advanced thumb exercise]

The etude for this lesson was composed Auguste Franchomme. This etude was modified from the original in order to adjust it to the level of this lesson. It is a piece that shows perfectly that there is no strict border between exercise and repertoire. Try to approach this piece as if you were to perform it in public.

Larghetto con dolore ♩. = 60

[Video 24.16: Caprice No. 9 by Auguste Franchomme]

The piece for this lesson – and the final piece in our 24 lessons! – is the famous Elegie op.24 by Gabriel Fauré.

It is one of the nicest short pieces written for the cello, yet one of the most demanding. In terms of intensity of expression, it is on the same level as the great concertos. However, it is still fairly nice to play, proving that Fauré understood the cello very well.

In the melodic parts, focus on playing every note with a good sound. Take good care of the dynamics – the dynamic range in this short piece is enormous!

The faster bits in the middle section require good left hand skills. Practise slowly with the metronome!

Before getting started with the real piece (and as a tool underway), here are some exercises to prepare you:

108

Gabriel Faure

1845 - 1924

Molto adagio

[Video 24.17: "Elegie" by Gabriel Fauré]

Summary of Lesson 24:
- Shift exercise pattern 1
- Shift exercise pattern 2
- Advanced thumb exercise
- Caprice No. 9 by Auguste Franchomme
- Practise patterns for the Elegie by Grabriel Fauré
- "Elegie" op.24 by Grabriel Fauré

Martin Stanzeleit

Martin Stanzeleit is currently the principal cellist of the Hiroshima Symphony Orchestra. Furthermore, Martin Stanzeleit appears in numerous solistic concerts throughout the year, both as soloist with orchestra, and in recitals with piano. Besides his solo career, Martin Stanzeleit is dedicating his time to chamber music.

Martin Stanzeleit was born 1971 in Bamberg, Germany, into a musical family. Having started to play the violin at the age of three, he changed to the cello at the age of five.

After graduating high-school, he enrolled at the Folkwang University as a student of Young-Chang Cho, taking his exam with highest honors in 1995. He further studied with Janos Starker, Ralph Kirshbaum and Ivan Monighetti, before entering the soloist class at the Folkwang-University with Christoph Richter.

After graduating, Martin Stanzeleit became a member of the Royal Danish Orchestra, before following a request by the Copenhagen Philharmonic Orchestra to act as principal cellist under their chief conductor Heinrich Schiff. After giving his solo debut in Copenhagen in 1996, an enthusiastic critic of the biggest Danish newspaper wrote: 'Martin Stanzeleit gets the music to live and breathe... his playing is both ardent and ecstatic, full of lyrical refinement.'

In 2003, Martin Stanzeleit successfully launched the concert series "Only Chamber Music", which includes artists from the HSO as well as guest players.

His CD debut in Japan in 2010 on the acclaimed 'Exton'-Label won nationwide praise. Martin Stanzeleit is the author of several books on Japan and works as a regular writer for the National Japanese Broadcasting Company NHK. In 2011 he founded the Kammerphilharmonie Hiroshima, for which he acts as the musical director. The orchestra subsequently went on tour to Germany, with its concert in Berlin being broadcasted live by the German Radio DR. Martin Stanzeleit appeared as a soloist with the Hagen Chamber Orchestra, Hiroshima Symphony Orchestra, Hiroshima Wind Orchestra, Iida Symphony Orchestra, the Philharmonia Georges Enescu, the Burgas Symphony Orchestra and the Sliven

http://www.martinstanzeleit.com/eng/engindex.html

Chihiro Takeuchi

Chihiro Takeuchi is a part-time teacher of physics at Fukuoka University. She studied cello with Minoru Honda and Martin Stanzeleit.

http://www5a.biglobe.ne.jp/~takafami/takapi/celloschool/celloschool.html

24 Lessons   VOL.2
A Practical Method to Learn the Art of Cello Playing

Martin Stanzeleit and Chihiro Takeuchi

http://www.martinstanzeleit.com/24lessons/24lessons.html

Recording
Cloval Hall Sakurazaka Fukuoka Japan

Made in the USA
Coppell, TX
21 July 2023

19449748R00063